WRITE
BLOODY

SPILL
PRETTY

Arielle Estoria & Sarah Wallick

Write Bloody, Spill Pretty
Arielle Estoria & Sarah Wallick

Design: Andrea Cenon
Los Angeles, CA • andreacenon.com
Typefaces: Klimt, Nexa, and Lora

Printed in The United States

"Embracing the fullness of our humanity through words"

Dedicated to the souls whose presence
has lingered on our pens long enough
to draw out of us that which
we did not know was there...
especially all y'all who have no idea
these poems are about you.

With all our love,

places

places

20927

I'm walking up to
a front door again.

This is one I've never seen before.
I'm not alone, though.
Newfound kin, walk beside me.
Doorbell, disregarded.

Door, unlocked.
We walk right in, no hesitation
because there is no hesitation
when you know you're coming home.

Shoes, slipped off.
Fears, left outside
next to the welcome mat
because that invitation
isn't extended to them here.

As we step inside I hear
the most beautiful music playing.

Warm smile melodies dance with
harmonies of welcoming hugs
laughter repeats herself knowing
how wonderful she sounds as the chorus.

new names and histories
and futures and prayers
and worship and testimonies
write the rest of the lyrics.

I've no need to ask my kin
for the title of this song
because my heart is telling me
this is what Living Hope sounds like.

I'm only beginning to learn
this new song.
I cannot wait until I am able
to sing it by heart

This body

We are curvy,
with more handles than we know how to love
we are thighs without gaps
highlighted cheek bones still little girl round

We have been wrestling with these bodies
treating them more like battle grounds than temples
more temporary homes than lighthouses
we have pinched, pulled and tugged
allowed shattered mirrors to blind our perceptions

We have squirmed in this skin for too long
so let's make a pact,
that we would love these curves,
these thighs and every handle
that we would tuck grace filled declarations
into every part of these bodies

That we would begin each day
with mantras in the mirror,

THIS BODY IS MINE
This body is beautiful

This body is mine
This body is beautiful

refuse to be shamed into covering these curves
as if they were disposable pieces
or X marks for digging out unwanted treasures
to make someone else more comfortable
our bodies were not made to make others feel comfortable

These bodies are temples
with sacred novels and holy scriptures etched into our bones
built to hold more passion than a human being can fathom

You were made for glory, the human epitome of light
a spirit so vast that it had to be contained behind flesh
to tone down its brilliance

These bodies are glitter
and yet we wake up and before they even have a chance to breathe,
and convince them that they are wrong
that they have failed at their chance
to be something worth holding
worth loving

These bodies have done us nothing but good
they have loved us through every toilet kiss and skipped meal,
cried tears for every time we compared them to others,
wrapped their arms around us when everything else felt distant

these bodies, have always been faithful
so I think it's time we returned the favor

Say it with me,
This body is mine
This body is beautiful
This sweet body is mine and the entirety of this body is beautiful

Waiting Room (pt. I)

waiting rooms
can be slightly
horrific experiences
for impatient people

I don't want to
make this prettier
than the scary
it actually is

I'm an impatient person
I'm in a waiting room
yes, physically, I
couldn't even open the door

the first time I tried
unable to muster
the strength to try again
someone else buzzed me in
what a cruel favor

I'm an impatient person
I'm in a waiting room
yes, in this season of life
liminal spaces

seem to be
the only thing these
trembling knees are
capable of standing in

feeling like I wear
lost and scared like
the worst of sunburns
skin that covers me

yet takes painstakingly
too long to strip itself away
leaving me tender and
easily susceptible to pain

Parked

One night, I felt restless
so i drove up the nearest winding road
found an outlook spot and parked.

shortly after, a man came tapping on my window,
asked if It was okay if I moved somewhere else
so that he could take a shower
and if I wanted to come back in 15 minutes, I could

in that moment,
i felt my privilege start the ignition of my car, lights off
i felt humility grab hold of my heart
and squeeze it just enough for me to feel its tug
in that moment, gratitude played one too many songs in my head
and I counted every blessing I could remember

maybe I should have timed the 15 minutes,
gone back and asked for his name
ask to hear a version of his story
he would feel comfortable sharing with a stranger
ask where he was and who he is becoming

in that moment,
I realized how quickly we are to ignore
human beings when we are faced
with not enough similarities
to make us feel comfortable

I wondered how many voices
have I drowned out in my discomfort
without even knowing
would I be able to meet them again one day?
would I be able to look them in the eyes,
tell them my name and ask them for theirs
and hope that even for a moment they felt known, felt seen
instead of hurried past or ignored

do their stories start to forget the tone of their voices
because no one asks them what they sound like anymore?
does their passion no longer make home in their blood,

tap on their ribcage and give their heartbeat something to echo?
if they were seen by me or by someone else,
would it bring the music back?

I have passed one too many skid rows
to ignore the extent of lost numbers in humanity
they haven't gone anywhere so why do we keep writing
"non existent" on still breathing bodies?

What if we stopped hastily moving
from one destination to another,
and instead acknowledged the breathing beings
ignored all around us

they are not threats,
they are not inconveniences,
they are human
some of them wanting to simply be left alone
and some hoping they can slip their way back into frame and be seen again
hoping to spill answers to questions people stop asking them
how are you?
who are you?
what are you doing?
where are you going?
what's your name?

My name is Arielle,
I know you have a story, maybe you've lost it
or maybe you've forgotten how it sounds
Let me help you find the tune

Stay

"On your mark! Get set!"
gone

I can still hear
the starting line gunshots
ringing in my ears
every race I've ever run
flashes before my eyes

I am great at getting out of the gates
I guess it's no surprise
I ran track in high school

I can't ever seem to escape
these cycles – I mean circles
around this track

repeating my past patterns
perpetually propelling
these feet forward even when
they should've stayed put

I'm at the starting line again
the opportunity to run
has presented itself
like a broken record
that loves to be replayed

coaxes this voice to sing along
with the melody it plays
melodies motivated by fear
seducing my feet to believe
they were born to harmonize
in the key of moving on quickly

that staying put
has always been offered
at a cost my feet
should never be willing to pay

so they harmonize
sing love songs to concrete
because they yearn to replicate
it's ability to allow other things

to touch itself
without ever penetrating it
leaving itself unaffected
by the footprints of people

who are only interested
in using it as a means to the end
their feet will finally choose
to rest on

and all of sudden

I'm back at the starting line
except this time I've made enough
laps around this track to know better

than to start a race
my desire to be known by others
will always outlast me in
no matter how far away I get

from relationships – I mean starting lines,
I always find myself
back at the beginning

I can still hear the
starting line gunshots
ringing in my ears
every race I've ever run
flashes before my eyes

I don't remember when it started
I suppose that's irrelevant now

considering I've still
got this urge to run,
run fast and far

to where this heart
can't be penetrated
permeating through these bones

pulsing through these veins
but they're being challenged
by feet weighed down with subversion
against their history
of being motivated by fear

this time is different
I've caught myself
mid warm-up

I'm still here, not gone,
not yet at least

"On your mark! Get set!"
stay

purpose

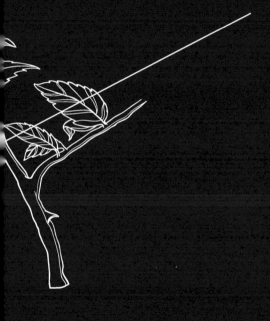

purpose

No Class for Calling

It's been a year since walking across that stage
grabbing my non-diploma with a smile as big
as if it knew what completion was

when people ask me what it is I do,
I have summed it up in one response,
"it depends on the day"
and it's true because it does

Because some days "work"
means find a coffee shop and make it your home
when you return the next two nights,
the barista will say to you "Hey, welcome back!"
and you no longer have to type the wifi password
because all your electronics just know

You will lean over to the person next to you who is wondering
if the wifi is public or not and whisper,
"the password is cup of grace"
And she smiles like maybe you work there or
maybe you're just there too much but she gets it

And some days
"work" is handing people cups of coffee
because you know what that sweet nectar does to you at 2pm
keeps you pushing till 6 or 10 or 12

And afterwards, you run home to shower
because you have a show that night
And you listen to your own voice through your speakers
and talk to yourself in the car
because you just memorized the poem
you wrote last night, this morning

And you tell people that they're magic and worthy
And that there is a God who loves them very much

And when they come to talk to you, you smile,
And say thank you over and over
You give them the bookmark with your face on it
and tell them to keep in contact
And they do

And now you are personality,
brand,
business,
and the product

And one time I had someone ask me
what classes I took to get where I am today
I laughed and told her honey,
there are no classes that can teach you
how to fulfill a purpose you thought
didn't belong to you in the first place
I told her that there are no classes for calling
you just have to say yes

and He does the rest

we spend so much time in classes, our faces in books
trying to understand what was already written next to our names
before we even grasped the idea of breathing

A year ago I said yes,
I'll let go and let you work
I will let my type A need for a plan
take a back seat
I said you move and I'll wait
I said you work and I'll walk

During a month where I could not
pay bills or buy groceries,
I told my father through tears
that I would not have chosen this life
I would not have chosen uncertainty,
I would not choose to be human tornado
unsure of what ground feels like

But I ran from this for too long and eventually,
Well, a friend once told me that your art makes space for you

It opens up its doors and says **finally,**
Because you stopped running
And you let the craft grab you
and you're terrified because it doesn't quite make sense
But it's yours

Above all you could ever ask or imagine
That's what He promised

Everyday you will need a reminder
everyday you will wake up questioning
why you work four jobs just to sustain one person
there will be no reasonable answer
None of this will make sense
There will be no step by step plan
There will simply be a trust me - I got this

Slam Poet

When your kindergarten
teacher asked you
*"What do you want to be
when you grow up?"*

I bet you didn't answer, "A *slam poet!*" Me neither...

because tying your shoes
and playing duck, duck goose
were more important and
you had yet to experience

the kind of tragedy
only a stage and mic
can save you from

during the days when you
wore overalls and learned
to tie your shoes – or didn't
so you could have those curly laces

when it was more desirable
to hold class pets than pens
grip monkey bars than paper
I never thought the diary

my dad gave to first grade me
would awaken an insatiable
appetite for writing,
but here I am

somewhere I never
planned to be,
but now I see
it was everywhere
I was meant to go

I don't prefer the term poet,
but it seems simpler
than telling someone

I sling shot verbs into motion
use a bow that shoots metaphors
into brains so they can
understand the symbolism

I construct soliloquies like
ancient kings cownstructed castles:
with tall towers revealing
my vocabulary's glory

while still being able
to keep everything I don't
want people to know
hidden behind its walls

but that might overwhelm someone
who just wanted to know if I was a poet

I'd still rather tell them
I'm a wordsmith
slicing through stories like
biologists slice through cells

but instead of biology
this is etymology
a wordsmith wielding weaponry
to create amazing alliterations any
Da Vinci would be jealous of

properly forging figurative language
with common day occurrences
breathing life into the feelings
others cast into caskets
because they never knew
how to put them into words

I figure that might also overwhelm someone
who just wants to know if I'm a poet

but this isn't for them; this one
is for *us slam* poets
we who can withstand
the refining fire

of five random judges
and emerge with
a more regal rhyme scheme
the next time

us slam poets who don't do it for the scores

but do it to lace lyrics to the
song of another person's heart
so they can finally find their own voice
and know they are not alone

slam poets are everything
every kid wanted to be
when they were growing up
we act as astronauts

when we take our audiences
to another space
we are the police
who arrest every crook

who stole a piece of you
when they tried to
silence your dreams

we're even your presidents
when we can create
policies with the placement
of our punctuation

we're the Olympic gold medalists
who know how to hurdle past
the pain of losing loved ones
and finish poems

in three minutes
like they're races
to prove we're the ones
running things

we're even the
international relations translators
because poetry has never been
confined to a single language

we're the artists who have
used all of our five senses
to create the mental images
your blood has been painting

across the skies of your veins
every stroke of our diction
we paint across the
canvas of your heart
reminds you you're alive

flash back to the
three foot seven inch tall me
to the days of remembering
six was afraid of seven
because seven ate nine

playing kickball at recess
until my navy blue pants were dirt brown
I can see why I never
worried about answering

my kindergarten teacher
when she asked me
what I wanted to be
when I grew up

I didn't want to overwhelm her

Feel That?

When we live in a world that forces us to believe
that we will only be good enough,
worth it, successful or loved
if we are everything but who we already are

Continuously being stripped of our own blueprints
that were handcrafted into every part of these bodies
with fearfully and wonderfully made tattooed on their edges

Place your hand over your heart,
do you feel that?
that is purpose

And as long as it is beating,
as long as you can hear life pumping through your veins
no one can take that away from you

Do everything you can to spread beauty
blow it out of your hands like c o n f e t t i
and never be afraid of the way that it shines

Never be afraid of the way that you love
or how your passion tends to rise from the depths of you

Do not bite your tongue when there are novels
desperately waiting on the edge of your mouth

You are purposed
and you are worthy
You are loved
and you are good enough

Place your hand over your heart,
do you feel that?
that's what purpose sounds like
memorize its beat
and give yourself permission to dance to its rhythm

as long as you can hear life pumping through your veins
no one can take that away from you

Grab their hand,
place it over their own heart
and tell them to dance

Prisoner

I don't have to be a slave forever
got truth buried deep in these divine letters
holy words leaping off pages
into my dirtied hands

introducing themselves as instructions
for how to pick the very locks
I imprisoned myself in
these words feel uncomfortable

like shoes six sizes too small
uncomfortable, like truth
like too many people
in an elevator at one time

uncomfortable like these words
want me freed more than
the hands they leapt into
why won't I let myself go free?

pleaded with God to let them go free
let faith ring these vocal cord alarms
soon sirens shot out of these lips
sounding like grace bear hugging
the undeserving as I asked
God to forgive me too

these sirens soon stopped,
knowing He was indeed
faithful to forgive
these folded hands then learned
how to open themselves again
knees foolishly and prematurely

broke up with the ground
they'd rested on
feet taught themselves
how to walk away
with chains still choking their ankles

taught themselves
how to dance to the sound
of shackles swaying in gusts of guilt

distracting themselves to avoid
admitting they were still imprisoned
by the weight of this memory
that forgot to remind me
to forgive myself

why won't I let myself go free?

Community at the Cross

"Have the courage to trust love one more time,
and always one more time." – **Maya Angelou**

the scene was quite strange
roman soldiers suspended
His body on two wooden beams

yet He, whilst in agony
suspended any concern
for Himself

broke through the blood,
sweat, and rejection
pouring down His face
with eyes less concerned
with His own marred appearance

more concerned with
meeting the eyes of
those whom He loved
packed a lifetime of provision
into seven simple words

"When Jesus saw his mother
and the disciple whom he loved
standing nearby, he said to his mother,
'Woman, behold, your son!'
Then he said to the disciple,
'Behold, your mother!'
and from that hour the disciple
took her to his own home"

family, there was
community at the cross

I'm worried we have
cultivated selective hearing
hear the call to pick up
our cross and carry it

but somehow miss the reality
that picking up our cross
includes picking up the
community that comes with it

we do not have the right
to choose only one

God was not joking
when He proclaimed we
are made in His image
yet we seem to forget He
is the very image of community

always fellowshipping with
the Son and Holy Spirit

family, have you forgotten
that community is worth it?

Jesus, the Lamb of God who
loved us more than His own life
loved us so much
He gave us each other

community is not a chore
community is a privilege
do not allow your ears
to unselect this truth

it is glorious, family!
yes, it is messy
yes, it sometimes hurts,
a lot

I know very well
community can hurt like hell

hurt like best intentions
and misunderstanding
bare knuckle boxing

hurt like the hands that
taught me how to break
down my own walls
breaking my heart too

hurt like vulnerability
placing itself in the
hands of sinners
family, we are clumsy

sometimes abandon the very
things we should be protecting

yes, community
can hurt like hell
but it also
heals like heaven

heals like hands
refusing to let go
no matter how far
our fears force us to run
from the people we need most

heals like forgiveness
like unconditional
heals like prayers that
are not familiar with ceasing

like the freedom
of being fully known

and still being fully loved
heals like the sound of
promised covenant drowning out
the cries of our own fear
that people will eventually
turn their backs on us and walk away

family, I pray we would
hear the glory and worthiness
hidden in the beckon to community
spoken over a mother and disciple

by the quivering lips
of our Savior as He hung
reviled and suffering
on a cross, for us

let us never forget
there exists *immeasurable*
JOY in community!

that it is home to
strength beyond our own
and filled with God's
inheritance in the saints

Mary and the beloved disciple
walked all the way to the cross
and Jesus, knowing
they hadn't even walked into
their darkest hour yet,

turned His agony into
an afterthought
shed suffering so simply
so He could clothe
His every movement
in compassion

reached down with kindness
and entered into their suffering
so they wouldn't feel alone

we were never created to live life alone

if you believe in Jesus Christ,
family, do you know that truly
believing the gospel means
more than believing God's ability
to transform you?

to truly believe the gospel
means to also believe it for others
and learning to trust its ability
to transform others into people
who will know how to love you

NOT perfectly, but as best
as our clumsy and
redeemed hands can

family, will you believe with me
that the gospel is greater
than our fears of commitment?

that it drowns our past baggage
in seas of grace and sweeps
clean slates and faith onto
the shores of our future?

Abba is calling us to community
do you hear him?

then let us rejoice
that the gospel
enables us to answer!

let us rejoice that we,
often inadequate and
always imperfect sinners,
now receive the opportunity

to be known as His disciples
when we love one another

Radiant

I think it's time
you danced a little harder
dreamed a little bigger
laughed a little fuller

I think it's time you sang at the top of your joy
and cried at the depths of your sorrow

I think it's time you lived and lived full

Time you shook off the haters or whoever
and walked as if you just discovered rockets
on the bottom of your feet
proof, that your destination was never this place to begin with
I think it's time you explored the universes in your own galaxy,
let yourself be captivated with your own shooting stars

Have you noticed that you trail glitter and gold everywhere you go?
and there is a radiance about you that cannot be described

I think it's time that we allow the wind
to kiss these wings

I think it's time that we lived so boldly
in this skin that we can call home
that we encourage others to walk just as bold

I think it's time you held yourself a little closer
and stopped filling empty spaces with empty people
I think it's time
you stopped being so afraid
of your own reflection in the mirror

our bodies need us to hold them, to love them tenderly and fervently
to look at our reflection without wincing
they need us to say,
"Today body, you did good"

we've stopped celebrating our bodies
because we're too busy punishing them

be the voice in the back of your own head
that reminds you of all the truths you need to keep
say them over and over again
until they become the spine
that makes you stand taller

Have you noticed that despite every pinch and pull---
that you are loved by the Creator of this universe
and He whispers,

I want all of you
every part that you think you can hide from me
when I am the one who gave them life in the first place
I don't see flaws my child, I just see radiance

Pangea

I look down
feet
still wanting to run
farther
and closer
at the same time

tensions arising
fighting
like tectonic plate movements
must be careful

not to end up
in two
auctioning off
fragments of myself
that do not cost me anything

because they give
no one
the complete map
to this soul

mustn't allow myself
to tire
of being Pangea

still looking down...
pockets full,
ready to pay the cost
of letting Pangea spill
back into my namesake

let these fears
tectonic plate move
as far away
as they want

I will not go with them this time

I was never made
to be continents
I was made to be
whole

to be inhabited,
searched and known
mapped out
never uncharted territory

I've wasted too much
time trying to transform
the home in these hands
into vacation destinations

wasted years training myself

to feel uncomfortable
when others stay
longer than a week

I've heard travelers
spend nights tenderly
trying to whisper the
fear out of my fingers

only to whisper
independence and
trust issues
back at them

tonight I will quiet
these lips longing
for the false sense of safety
hidden in isolation

I will not hiss back

I will unwind the trust issues
choking out the
authentic longevity
in my relationships

I will reassure my heart
until it learns
to honor the home
in these hands

I am done
drifting away
from the Pangea
mapped in my DNA

I am learning to cherish
the look of safety
in the eyes of others
when they realize

I will let them stay
as long as they like
and will let them learn
e v e r y
i n c h
of my Pangea

abba

abba

Ab•ba
/ ˈäbä,ˈabä /
noun
1. A tender, informal way a child would refer to their father.
2. (in the New Testament) an intimate term for God as father

Sincerely, Misunderstood God

I wrote you this letter
hoping it would somehow
find its way into your hands
I would've given it to you in person,

but I haven't seen you in a while
you stopped coming around
like the ocean suddenly
became allergic to sand

my shore hasn't seen
you wave hello in
I don't know how long

I hear it's because you think
I'm allergic to your mistakes
someone told you they saw Me
preparing for when I'd have to

put up with your failures
by drinking an entire
bottle of Benadryl as if

Spring birthed you into the air
along with the rest of her pollen
and you were nothing more
than something I was being forced

to endure for a season
you've been lied to – I love you
like Spring is my favorite season
because of you

love you like
everlasting to everlasting
because I am everlasting
like the word orphan

will never again root itself
in the soil of your identity
you are mine
your heart: the garden

I died to ravish with streams
that will not run dry
and food that will not perish

I want to miracle grow you
from the cracks
of this broken world
into the tree that will
yield its fruit

that will not wither
I won't let you wither
no matter the weather

I will carry you

will you trust my arms?
when every second guess
screaming inside of you
stems from your fear

that I will drop you
everything you've ever done
branching off to bloom doubt
in your darkest of nights

in those moments
you've promised to take
to your grave, so afraid
someone would ever unearth

the secrets you've buried deepest
stop hiding the shovel - I love you
my Son sings salvation
sonnets over you

but your eyes tell me
the only voice you can hear
is satan telling you
I've been keeping track

of how often I forgive you
like a prisoner drawing
tally marks on his cell wall

counting down the days
until his sentence is over
when reality is that every
tally mark I've ever made

has been an expression of my delight
in your childlike faith to
trust Me with more of you
will you trust Me with all of you?

or have you just been praying
I have been pretending
you haven't sinned against Me
trying to make Myself believe

I didn't see you at Calvary mocking Me
I need you to know I heard
the contempt in your voice
when you yelled, "Crucify Him!"

I saw the rebellion in your eyes
when you nailed Me to the cross
I would recognize those eyes anywhere

not because I've been

keeping records but because
I created those eyes

knit you together
in your mother's womb
carefully crafted your soul
specifically to love and
be loved by Me

I need you to know
I am not numb nor
blind to your sins
because I need you to know

I love you, still, in spite of them
it's true I feel the offense
of the pride in your heart
when you run from Me

but I still want
that very heart for my own
sent My own Son for you
asked Him to take your place

extend grace though you
didn't deserve it
the greatest exchange
turning every sinner to saint

My desire is never to condemn you
I desire to forgive you, always
until you are reconciled back to Me
this is the God I am
with arms that will carry you
they are recklessly relentless in
their pursuit of your trust

you are not orphan
you are beloved daughter
you are precious son

I am *Abba*, **Refuge**
not here to condemn you
I am here to rescue you

will you trust me if I tell you
it's never too late to run home?

You First

We can tell him that we love him
And every time he will respond with,
"I loved you first"

There will be no pingpong of language,
or a guessing game of who will hang up first

There is simply no competing with, *I loved you first*

This love for us paid with a price
that we could not live long enough to even try and repay

I loved you first
Formed before we even knew what love could look like

I loved you first
freely given with no strings attached

I loved you first
a love exhaled into your very being

I loved you first
a love with no limits, no restraints

Imagine being loved before anyone earthly knew you would exist

before you were a squirming ray of life in her womb

daily He declares, daily He shows

I loved you first

there simply is no competing with that, it graciously just is

He Is

To have a relationship with someone means to know them
know the entirety of their making, know why and how they are wired
to be in relationship with someone, means to know them

I AM the bread of life
his sufficiency enough
for the appetite of these bodies
and the needs of these spirits
knowing that he is and will be

I AM the light of the world
Darkness has no place where I reside
If you dwell here in the type of light that only I can provide
You will never walk blindly
I will guide you,
direct you through each valley and mountaintop
because before every person I have sent to guide you
I was and will be
before and after them

I AM the gate and the shepherd
Daughter and Son I will call you by name
I will open pastures for your life dripping in purpose
I will never leave nor forsake you
I invite you in not for momentary visits, but to stay and to dwell
These gates are always open, always home

I AM the resurrection and the life
the breath in your lungs
turning dry bones into new creations
Yes you, though fearfully and wonderfully made
were formed from ashes and will return to ashes
But through me yes because of me
death has lost its sting!

I AM the way, the truth, and the life
child seek me and rest assured you will find me

If you know me—truly know me
You will not be the same
because this knowledge of me
will change you, shift you, wreck you
from the inside out
and from the inside out will come your fruit
your outward expression of knowing me from internal depths

I am the true vine
the everlasting vine
wrapping myself around your very being
from your ribcages, to your hands

Abide in me, **remain in me**

You are always human doing
but here—in this vineyard of knowing me
Be still

These statements are not empty statements,
they are loaded declarations
of who Jesus was, is and will be

little letters addressed to us so that in return,
we understand who we are as well

To know him
is to love him

To know him
is to reflect him

I am,
I am,
I am

64

I closed my eyes
and bowed my heart
on bended knee in humility
I sought the King of all kings

as I waited in the quiet
my harried soul He stilled
it was then, "I *saw the Lord*

sitting upon a throne
high and lifted up
and the train of His robe
filled the temple."

His voice spoken like trumpets
I praised in symphonies
His presence dripped drops of jasper

shined with a carnelian coloration
a beauty indescribable
an unmatched magnificence
multiplying my mind's motivation

to never forget what I'd seen
He was surrounded by 24 thrones
and elders who wore crowns and robes
but His throne shone

like it was unmarred by the scars
of His creation's rebellion
it was wrapped in ribbons
of rainbows radiating emeralds
it was as if I was seeing
green for the first time

as I drew nearer
my heart began to beat
like the flashes of lightning
and peals of thunder

that erupted in rumbles
from His throne
I was like a child
counting the seconds between
each flash because I knew
just like lightening and thunder
the quicker my heart beat
the closer I was to eternity

I found myself drowning
in holiness and grace
but completely content
with the idea of never

breathing again if it meant
I could stay there forever

suffocating in the sea of crystals
set to reflect the perfection
of a love unchanged by rejection

I told myself not to speak
finally and fully aware of how
unclean my lips really were
I began to cower in shame

but a seraphim flew near
touched my mouth
with a burning coal
and said my sin was atoned for

looking up with new eyes
I saw before the throne
were burning torches of fire

seven flames burning brighter
with every passing second
flames of light consuming
every one of my attractions to darkness

like they were nothing more than
molecules of oxygen waiting
to be used for a greater purpose

"holy holy holy"
the symphonies of
perfect praise grew louder
I drew closer, now standing

next to four living creatures
each with six wings
eyes all around and within

as if to prove the inability
of any human mind
to fully comprehend or describe
the true definition of divine

I joined in, knelt down
and asked God to compose me
however He saw fit
little did I know

He'd been outlining me
to be His masterpiece
since before the beginning of time
I never realized

He had transformed
my heartbeat into the bass
my voice into the harmony
to match the melody of voices

already proclaiming
"Worthy are you our Lord
and God to receive glory
and honor and power"

His whispers provided
the instrumental
laying the foundation
for every breath

He placed in my chest
to become another lyric
in the psalm He
is writing me to be

and just like creation
He spoke me into new life
with one word I became
His living poetry

published with the sole purpose
to share my sonnet of salvation
revealing His glory to all the nations

I Will Not Wait

I have never become
so intimate
with the color brown

swatches of tan
and dust coverings
cloak my vision

no matter which way I look
desert storms surround me
on every side the way I wish
Your voice would

my God,
I cannot hear you
over the howling silence
over the slander whose echoes
reach for me from lands I have left
out of obedience to You

these echoes burrow
themselves in my ears
try to whisper
of the desert's curse

but I will not wait
until I can hear Your voice
to call to mind the way
Your presence led my kin

in these same wildernesses
cloud by day and fire by night
my God,
you surround me
like I wish you would

Your voice still speaks
calms desert storms like
they are the raging waters
Your disciples feared

I will not trust these echoes
I will trust my kin
trust your word

and rejoice over the way
You show up in the desert
like I'd never truly
beheld your beauty
until this storm

Salt & Sea

When God calls you to the edge
of unfamiliar shores,

Take in salt

Take in sea

Take in peace

And just breathe

watch the waves
and know that they are
no bigger than their creator

Do not be afraid,
this is just the beginning
of the greatest adventure
written by the hands of a great God

Unfeigned Petition

I lay everything at your feet,
every broken piece of me

I press these knees into this holy ground
pressed into the sweetest surrender

I pray that you would meet this brokenness
with your wholeness

that I would unclench this pride
and inhale your humility

Father if you must, please break me
strip me of everything that does not radiate you

Father speak and I will stay
rested in your grace
overwhelmed by your mercy

And if I ever thought I could do this on my own,
how mistaken I was and will be
if I do not let you stop me in the midst of my human doing
and bring me to stillness
a stillness that waves over worry
and floods over doubt

Lord,
you are my Provider, my Redeemer
my yesterday, today and tomorrow

I can quote scripture,
scream at the top of my lungs about your goodness
but how empty are these declarations if not weighted with your truth

I will hush every hypocritical soapbox response from these lips
I will be every bit of broken imperfection,
if it helps me come to terms
with the elegant rawness of my own humanity
come to terms with the worthy in my flaws
that you remind me of daily
and still you invite me in, you invite me to come
flawed and all
broken and torn

I am speechless
when in the presence
of your overflowing grace

So when my words become few,
and the pretty has been stripped from my tongue
let only these remain,

Lord you are faithful,
Lord you are good,
Lord you are constant
and you're here with me now

you're here with me now

As Long As It Takes

prostrate is becoming
the dearest of friends
with these knees,

this face, these hands
that no longer have any idea
what to do with themselves

when they have been
grasping for hours
in vain.

Your presence
evades these outstretched
and empty palms
while this heart
barely beats,
begging, beseeching

Your presence
to no longer tarry
in the distance
every moment You delay

these barely beating chambers
become further hollowed out
by their misplaced
fear of abandonment

I'm scared
of how swiftly
numbness cloaks
this heart

the way intimacy looks
more like an old photograph;
a sunlight-faded, dust-covered
token of a past my memory
can no longer recall on its own

You feel far
like other side
of this mountain

like I have not yet
persevered long enough
to see the light
at the end of this tunnel

but I am learning
my perception
of Your nearness
does not dictate
my need to rejoice

see You are faithful

even when I can't feel you

when this heart
is cloaked in numbness
I will rejoice over the way

You show Yourself faithful
in the fact that
I feel grieved
by this numbness

Abba, You are worthy
of every cry offered up
as a sacrifice
of my independence

even when my ears cannot hear Your reply

so I will sit
until I learn the
closeness of breath, the
nearness of indwelling

I will wait here,
for You

no matter
how long it takes
no matter
how long I mistake
perfect timing for tarrying

I am choosing
to trust the way I feel
will never affect
who You actually are

You are close as breath
You dwell within me,
even when I feel numb
I only pray, Father,

for patience to embed itself
in every letter of my name
so that when You call to me
You hear her too

hear how dedication
seeps into every consonant
hear perseverance
dig deep into each
of these vowels

I want my name and patience
to roll off Your tongue
like they never knew

what it was like
to be without the other

I pray
I would wait for You

pray for Your voice
to one day become louder
than every other voice
in this head

 hold more sway
than every other feeling
vying for my attention,
every lie fighting
for my allegiance

I've heard it said
You speak in the stillness
and can be found
in the whisper

so I am here
and I will wait
as long as it takes
I will wait and trust

You will teach me
the way silence
can speak volumes
how sweet whispers
quiet every other noise

of numbness'
inability to outlast
Your pursuit of this heart

him

him

Thief

Thief, *noun*

"a person who steals another person's property especially by stealth and without using force or violence."

it's been somewhere
close to 1,460 days
since our chapter ended
yet you still have the audacity

to wear criminality with grace
steal pieces of me
I promised myself
I'd keep for another

I never invited you
back in, which makes
me wonder if
you ever left

vacated the sheets
of my speech
cleaned out your mannerisms
from my closet

my mind then serves me
reality via memory
replaying the night
I asked you to walk away

my eyelids silently blanket
these eyes turned oceans
needing no aid to retrace
those weariness-filled crevices
beneath your eyes

nor to replay how I watched
them deepen in direct proportion
to my fear that I was
letting you in too close

my mind is not brave
enough to create the
memory of you leaving
leaving me no other option
but to accept this reality

which makes me feel crazy
because I swear I can still
hear the echo of you closing
the door behind you

when you walked out
of this relationship
yet you continue to
burglarize my speech

invade my conversations
loot my words
until the only ones left
have your fingerprints
all over them

you really are
a terrible criminal

you borrow my thoughts
with no intention of
giving them back because
you think they look better
dressed in you

you've confused corridors
of this heart with vacant lots
begging you to make
your home here

troubling my pen
for one poem too many
troubling my eyes to
abandon their hope of respite

when it's 1:14am and
my roommate is asking
if I'll go to bed soon, but I
can't give her an honest answer

because I don't know
if these pens will ever
stop bleeding your name
and I'm desperate enough
to abandon the hope of respite
for the hope of an answer

I just want to stop
writing poems about you
when you don't even
think about me anymore

hate how my words
wear beautiful when
they decide to date you
for a couple bars

you don't deserve
my best lines
but these memories refuse
to stop giving them to you

got me asking why they refuse
why my neck still checks for
your car when I roll past your block
every time I take a trip home

maybe these poems never get
finished and my thoughts
never evict you because
this was never about you
in the first place

you are merely a tool
they choose to use
to dig for something deeper

it's been somewhere
close to 1,460 days
since our chapter ended
and I have no difficulty
admitting we are both very
different people now

the more I discipline myself
to sit in this crime scene of an
empty hole you left behind
connecting clues to give me
the evidence I need so I
can honestly say it isn't
you I want back

you are merely the tool these pens
use to dig for something deeper
so I can remember once again
what it feels like to be fully known

you are no thief
you are puppet
every physical feature
and mental characteristic

my diction delights
to digress on
was only a mask
so who is the thief?

these pens for stealing ink
to keep you alive in my poems?
perhaps these hands for
selfishly clinging to
distractions disguised as

wrap around porch smiles
and hands that held like home
parts of you that were
never meant to belong to me

I owe you an apology
you are not a thief
my heart,
my heart is the thief

stealing my time, my conversations,
betraying itself by stealing my own
thoughts and dedicating them to you
though you have no interest in it

all so I could relive every
moment I lost myself
in being wholly known by you
that's all my heart has ever longed for

at the end of the day
that's all each of our hearts
has ever longed for

the kind of known that has sat beside you
and behind doors closed
to soften the blow of enduring
the raised and angry voices
of a family that was not his own

the kind of known that can drive, all night
no destination, no words
and still speak volumes
into a wearied soul

I apologize for ever calling you
thief when all you've ever done
was give me a small glimpse of the
eternity that has been set in my heart

this was never about
writing you out of my poems

this was always about
my heart stealing from itself
hoping it would one day
be caught red-handed

so it could open wide
my eyes to see what
I'd truly needed
all these years

it's been somewhere
close to 1,460 days
since our chapter ended
been somewhere
in this last poem

since I've finally
been okay that it,
that we, are over

Scribes

He knew how to string words
like Christmas lights
and my heart was a ready and eager pine tree
I wanted to be wrapped in his language
and made a memory in his wintertime
willing to let him unravel this soul of mine and intertwine his own
willing to be a blank page, if he only promised to fill me with his sweet nothings

I believed every trickle that slipped from his lips
because of the way his eyes could hold mine and keep me there

I was not prepared for the war that he would rage
with his ability to hold me so close yet keep me so far
an avalanche of truth that conveniently caused no damage to himself

I did not know how to protect myself from his verbal enticing
or the way he could bleed on a page so effortlessly
while I restricted everything like dainty tea sips from my mouth

All this and I'm still wondering,
why our fathers never warned us about poets

They cautioned us about boys with saggy pants,
those who did not know how to use the term "sir"
or shake a solid hand

But they never warned us about poets
the ones who have a thesaurus for a ribcage
instead of heartbeats, the click of typewriting
s p a c e d o u t
and
intentional

more than sweet talkers
They will hijak your creativity and call themselves your muse
so when they leave you are left speechless

You see poets; they don't try and fix you like the others,

Instead they articulate your existence in prose
and remind you that baby,
you're worth writing about
you're worth being told over and over again
you're worth permanent,
being held forever in the binding of a book that always reminds you
of every love that you fought and every love you wished would return

they kiss your intellect and delicately whisper to your emotions
reminding you that you are storm and you are beautiful

you are breathtaking and you are beautiful
you are shore and you are beautiful
you are grace and you are beautiful
You are inhales, exhales, silence and beautiful
With poets, you never have to say, *I love you*

instead you trace one another with your eyes
and memorize how the other breaths

and even if you didn't consider yourself a work of art before
once a poet has tiptoed on your heart strings
and once you have left your fingerprints on their thesaurus of a heart
you will always be a synonym for love

and no matter how much time has passed in-between,
they will always make a poem out of you

He'll Get There

He loves in the only way a young boy knows how
with distant parents both emotional and physical

He makes his own love language
and hopes someone is daring enough to understand

More geometry than science
He is wondering if triangles
are enough distance between three points
so as not to get close enough to hurt or be hurt

He has learned
Only distance
With words and with body

He has learned,
that spilled ink always leaves stains

Letting love slip from his mistakes
taking one day at a time
one heart at a time
one vulnerable escape of confession he can manage

He is not so heartless,
despite the persona he carries on his shoulders
they are just chips he's forgotten the need to shake off

He loves in a way that a little boy
learning all over again knows how
but eventually the man will grow to love
with less fear and more courage next time
And he will get there one day
but that does not mean that that love
will ever be for you

Afraid

I do not know
who you are
yet I am still afraid
of your very existence

afraid of the pain
you will cause
afraid of the pain
I will cause

afraid of how
I will let you in
allow you close enough
to hurt me
allow you close enough
to love me
love all of me

allow you to convince me
I am someone worthy
of being loved

I do not know how
you will accomplish such feats
I am only praying

you will wear patience
and perseverance like
your memory actually believes
finishing this race with me
would be worth it

I am always praying by the
time you ask me to go running
I will no longer be afraid

or at least that fear won't convince me
I am better off running alone

it's like I'm asking you not to leave
before you've even arrived
yet my request is muffled

never quite reaches your ears
over the sound of draw bridges
and entrances being closed shut

because all I've ever left you hearing
is your own innocent voice
echoing off the walls

I built around myself

How Do You Do It?

For the past three years,
we have tiptoed
and criss-crossed on each other's hearts,
Letting our emotions dance with no language
we have learned the art of breathing the other in
as if we've forgotten what it's like to inhale for ourselves

But then one of us stopped dancing
learned the pace of their own breath again
found someone else's to fall in sync with

I found myself still creating melodies
to a choreographed duo that no longer existed
because you held hands opposite to my own
in flesh and in demeanor

I have never been anything close to dainty
not blonde haired or porcelain
I have always been brick house
big enough to take more than myself in
Always managing to forget
that I was a home first and not vacation check in

you found something in her eyes
that reminded you of the way
the ocean would touch sand
and always come back
Reminded you of the way your hands
would brush mine
and always leave

You cannot write unrequited love letters and
not expect me to burn them into the bridges
I need to cross over

I admit,
Because secrets are a foreign concept
in this space we've formed
That I wanted you
from day one
wanted a history remake with our own skin
wanted you
mind, body and soul
I gave you poems and spilled ink
ignoring the fact that you were undeserving
Of these melodies

How do you do it?
manage to always get the best of me,
when I had every intention of giving you none

At the End of it All, it Was You

I've never been one
to remember her own dreams
to be honest
I like it this way

sunrises rob my memory
of the way the moon
kissed these eyelids closed
wooed this cerebral cortex into expression

but
there are always exceptions
you have always been
the most torturing exception

I can still feel the panic that
surged through my body
shot it upward
out of bed sheets
onto the floor

the morning I awoke
with the memory
of I'd dreamt of you

we weren't talking much
at the time
like we aren't now
I was memorizing

the first poem
I'd written about you
like I'm memorizing
the second one now

stages and coaches
have always fallen
for the way my pens
caress your name

requiring of me the
memorization and rehearsal
of a story I spent nights
crying out of my memory

I never could cry long enough
my body still remembers the panic
the way the floor made hard wood
feel like a stretcher

carrying my body
away from that
crime scene of bed sheets
I still remember the dream

I'm scared tonight

will be the night
my memory becomes
a repeat offender

tattooing your face
across the inside
of these eyelids

but I'm a poet
I've got deadlines
I've got a show to do
but I've also got this fear

of closing my eyes
long enough to give you
the opportunity to sneak in

I've been memorizing
and rehearsing the story
I gave up on trying to cry
out of my memory

I wonder if you, the reader,
have discovered the pitfall
of being a poet who processes
via pen and paper

I'm scared to death
my attempts to memorize
that poem will cause me
to dream of him again

so I've chosen to run
from the sweet nothings
whispered by REM cycles
by writing another poem

about him

Dear sunrise,
Please, please come quickly.

Lifeline – A Father

A father,
is more than a role
and not just a title
it is something that you carry on your shoulders
and in the soles of your feet,
proof of it resting on your tongue and dancing in your speech
the way you express,
the way that you love
it is the grace you extend in your hands
and the depth of your grasp

To be a father is more than to be present
to be a father is to live a life in complete and utter sacrifice
for the very people you brought into this world

Fathers, do not exasperate your children instead,
Train them and build them up in the instruction of the Lord
guide them on the path that you won't always be on

We don't always understand how important a father really is,
until he saves us in the moments we need it the most
until he makes us laugh in the times when no one else can
until he tells us how beautiful or handsome we are
until you have a conversation with someone
 and they tell you they never had one,
or never knew who they were

consider this a letter of gratitude,
for your guidance and for your instruction"
your quirks and your strange ways of loving
You complete us
in all the ways and places we did not know
we were not whole to begin with

Despite how old we may be,
there will be parts of you coursing through every part
of who we are

Every conversation
where we didn't always see eye to eye,
who you've raised,
who we are becoming
starts with who you are
and who you've shown us to be

We are walking bodies of both mother and father
showing you pieces of yourself
that maybe you've forgotten existed

You remind us there's no such thing
as dreaming too big
or loving too hard
that we are deserving of stories rich in purpose

Father,
earthly reflections of our Heavenly one

using everyday as an opportunity to show us
what a man should look like, what he should and should not say

I woke up one morning to a text from my father,
it read: "I'm proud of you, you are a beautiful spirit

I could say the same for him too,
because it's true you know
that the apple doesn't fall too far from this tree

Come To Me

come to me gently
come to me with your slow and steady
let it sunset over my future's horizon
until this fear is put to rest

come to me quietly
soft speech of actions and words
speaking one tongue kind of love
unassuming speech humming hope's anthem
throughout the hallways of these homes
we are becoming to one another

come to me bravely
with a spine-straight kind of love
with a heart brave enough to receive
my stand tall next to you 'cause
I'm proud to be with you kind of love

come to me
just as you are
bruises and broken and all
different humor and old soul and all
intricacies and unknowns and all
let us face each of these together
as one kind of love

never interested in perfection
as much as faithfulness kind of love
so come, come to me,
my love

her

her

Small

I walked into a store,
found a dress I thought was pretty
and headed to the dressing room

Before I was even able to grab the handle I heard,
"They run small"
behind me was the owner, eyeing the items in my hand
"They run small"
she repeated, smiled and walked away

They run small
They run small
They run small

I have never been small
And every moment where my body felt massive and unlovable
Every uncomfortable teenage year and jeans barely past my thighs
Came rushing back

No, I have never been small.
not these hips nor these eyes
not these thighs nor this gut

Not this mind that thinks in deep, full circles
not this heart that makes room for more people than there is space for
not these hands, that always find ways to hold on tighter
not these words that expand larger than this breath
And most days, these breaths take in more life than I can stomach

I have never really been synonymous with the idea of small
except for when it came to a battle of self reflections in a mirror
minimizing my worth so that it fit like lost treasure
in maps people stopped viewing as real anymore
tattered, washed up

We were not handcrafted
and life given
to be small

We were meant to love big and live bigger
refuse to be threatened by the small people will try to box us in
the same small that we sometimes box ourselves in

They run small,
was just supposed to be an informed commentary

So I took it, decided to do some informing myself
put the dress back on the rack
and refused to be threatened by the idea of small
because I was never meant to fit in that anyway

Because Tuesday

Because Tuesday.
Because you are worthy.
Because peonies.
Because love, compassion,
friendship eclipsed by sisterhood.

Because even though "because"
is rendered useless by this delivery
not needing a reason behind it,
we still love the way "*just because*"
gift wraps itself when delivered
by the lips of those we love.

Kim, you need no reason
to receive flowers.

You are worth far more than
late night trips across town
into the bed of someone

who does not know how
to receive the consuming
fire wrapped in grace
that is your soul.

Lay yourself bare in hands
that consistently confuse
protecting themselves with
choking life from others who
shine beautiful without them.

You shine beautiful, Kim.

The kind of beautiful
recognized by closed eyes
and searching souls.

You are not disloyal.
You are intelligent, empathetic.
You are proof that
strength and brokenness
are not mutually exclusive.

You, young lady,
are worth more than
feet unwilling to move
relationships forward because
they are frozen in their
fear of commitment.

Mouths causing the
kind of pain that leaves
you questioning your worth
because they have not
taken the time to learn
the trade of wordsmithing.

Not understanding how
to control the hurricane
Katrinas that are words,
like you do; as if you
were Katrina's lover.

Kim, what you are worthy of
is authentic love.

Love that knows no one
greater than this, that
someone lay down his
life for his friends.

Love that hears your soul
before you even speak a word.
You are worthy of
pure intimacy,

that is not self-seeking,
but seeks to
serve and protect.
I pray you will learn

to receive this service,
experience it invading
the parts of your soul
you have not let
another yet touch.

You will know your Maker
is asking for
your permission to enter,

His voice will sound
like the final breath
before death swallowed
our innocent Savior whole.

Your presence, Kim,
is sought after.

The whispers of your
speech are longed for
by the Creator that
knit you together in
your mother's womb.

He did not spend such
meticulous time on your
every feature to let you
slip away into the darkness

that is the temptation
to author your own ending.
He will never let go of you.

You deserve to be held on to.
More than being worthy of,
you have already received
this kind of love.
A love that delights

to surround and awaken
every fiber of your being
to the truth that you
are already fully known.

You need not ever seek
to be known by minds that
cannot comprehend all
of the purposeful intricacies
that make you who you are.

You have purpose.
You have dignity.
You have the chance of
redemption because of love.

Because mercy renews itself
every day like the sun does
its desire to rise.
I love you, *just because.*

Because He first loved me
and is teaching me every day
how to love you the same way.

Because Tuesday.
Because you are worthy.
Because peonies.
Because love, compassion,
friendship eclipsed by sisterhood.

Because even though "because"
is rendered useless by this delivery
not needing a reason behind it
we still love the way *"just because"*
gift wraps itself when delivered
by the lips of those we love.

Curse Words

plump
round
thicker
heavier
these curse words
cut into you so deep

it isn't your fault, though
I wonder if you remember
the moment
I turned my back on you

have you tasted the
abandonment in my disregard
in my allowing those curses
to cut you wide open
bleed you dry of worth and value

could you see the
hope in my eyes as
they evaded your questions
did this hope kill you
more than the curses have?

the way I hoped
that as I stripped away
my protection of you
let those curses cut deep

that they'd trim away
the pieces of you
I've always scorned

deciding whatever else
they robbed you of
in the process was a price
I was okay paying

forgive me,
dear body
dear, dear body
so soft and so strong

I'm so sorry for being
more grieved by the
descriptions of others
than by the way my eyes
desecrate you every morning

with eyes that curse you
because all I want
is what you were never
created to be

dear, dear body
so supple and so supportive

you've held me up
all these years
even as I tore you down

I've been abandoning
my responsibility to protect you
forgive me, please
let us begin again

I confess I do not know
how to handle you
how to behold you
the ways you deserve

but I want to learn,
teach me

dear, dear body
so forgiving and so faithful
teach me to reciprocate faithfulness
until desecration is a language
I have long forgotten

#Dressember2016

She dances
because she knows she is free

She laughs
because she knows she is loved

She creates
because she knows there are seeds
planted in the palms of her hands
whatever she touches will bloom

she has hope
because somewhere
someone believed in her

she twirls and she twirls
and she will keep on twilling

She is not weak, she is not vulnerable
She is tornado and beauty all wrapped up in one
Twirling and powerful
Twirling and magical

So she dances,
effortlessly and without fear
because at last, she is finally free

Feminist

You are not bossy.

You're not a threat.

You are not a ticking bomb.

You are not a volcano of unruly emotions.

You are not any name outside of the one given to you by birth.

You are not the fistful of apologies you stuff in your mouth

when you have absolutely nothing to be sorry for.

You are not less.

You are mountains crumbling into the sea

A powerful force

Darling, you are far from being less.

S.O.S.

I'm sorry
sorry for every time
I was hard on you
refused to drink in

the reality that
you are human
you are woman
and in this world,
that is no easy task

swallow the truth
that you are no less
broken than I am
and do not deserve

to be drowned
by standards my own
character could not
keep afloat in

I'm so sorry compassion
was consumed by waves
of hurt and bitterness
so blinded by

all the moments
I felt you were never
willing to acknowledge
that I lost sight of the shore

where you've been this whole time

where every word
that hurricane-exited
your lips and flooded
my heart with pain

has only ever been
your way of crying "S.O.S."

telling me that you,
you are hurting too
that hurricane
is the only language
you know how to speak

because that's
the only language
your own mother
ever spoke to you in

Exuding Glory

And she
with butterfly spirit
and grace led feet

She
built with worshipping hands

She
with her abundant love
and restless heart for doing

She
with her dreams lifted
like prayers and piano keys

She
first insecure and uncertain
then blooming and sure
walking boldly in her coat of calling
leading with her all pouring out of her in abundance

no longer timid,
no longer afraid
of the power in her hands
and the spirit in her voice
abandons human body every sunday
and enters in the sacred between heaven and earth

She is now an open door
the gates of Glory opening the moment her fingers touch ivory
carries this worship in her spine

there is no silent shaking from you now
only the rumbling of hell itself being unsettled
every time divinity escapes from your mouth

She, not just leader but orchestrator
embodying worship
moments of reverence
she has carried ministry within her backbone
and with an essence known as nothing but pure gifting
allows these gifts to be given back to her Creator

She allows open hands to carry this worship
through her veins, echoing through her heartbeat
her very breath becoming music
a whisper of glory escaping from her lips

and she with all butterflies and grace
is harp and dance
the sacred in between of heaven and earth
On sunday keys meet flesh
and tongue meets air

eyes closed
Let everything that has breath Praise the Lord
Yes, let everything that has breath Praise the Lord

River Beds

I've got earthquakes for eyes
exposing the faults in
the foundations of this body
too many cracks

crept in
made their home
in my self-confidence
earthquakes for eyes

looks of judgement
coursing across my countries
capable of causing the strongest
bridges-to-hope affirmations
to crumble in its wake

this thunderstorm tongue
does not wait it's turn
does not fear the quaking
has no respect for silence

amplifies every act of destruction
with a voice bellowing
labels of disdain
louder than anything
that would try to challenge it

follows with lightening strikes
of disapproval just to reveal
how much darkness
my continents are covered in

coming home to myself
has always been a storm

I owe it to myself
to now seek the restoration
of the mother in my nature
rediscover its ability to
express care in its caress
of my land's every curve

this will not come easy
I've been storm as long
as I can remember
but I owe it to my Father

the Creator of my
mountain top shoulders
and valley palms
these river beds for hips
and fertile soil knees

whispering reflections
of His image, which
He knit me in likeness of

I have always been His
I haven't always whispered like it

I am His
and I finally want nothing more
than to learn to care for this reflection
like Him too

XOXO

I hope that you're not afraid to show up for yourself, or for other people.
Today, I hope that you are not afraid to let people show up for you
that you would unfold and flourish into this day effortlessly
I hope today, you realize what a victory it is that you are alive and breathing
we only want to celebrate the big most days,
we shake life and demand it to give us monumental
not even realizing that it gives us tiny victories and confetti parties everyday

so often we miss them because of how insignificant they seem
but only because we deem them to be insignificant

I hope you do not see yourself as insignificant
I hope today you are not afraid to be seen
I hope today you dare to see others

you can save a life doing that you know?
reminding people that they're needed here.
So this is my reminder to you: you're needed here
please, please realize how monumental it is that you are here

You are more galaxy built than anything else
vast and absolutely captivating
your very existence is a miracle in itself

An Ode to the Women

you have never been
so beautiful to me

the way God
tenderly tucked
each of you into my life
without me even noticing

desiring to fill each
of my shortcomings
with your strength and grace
take my needs
and carve them

into the deepest of valleys
so I could learn
the taste of your
rushing-river love

which is not afraid
of my fault lines
nor hindered by
the jagged edges of
this rocky soil soul

your streams of forgiveness
eroded the stone of my heart
whispered trust into my rib cages
until they were able to reverberate the

ba-boom,
ba-boom
of a heart of flesh
back into our relationships

I promise to never
abandon my awe
over the ways your hands
cling to me

like roots wanting to outgrow
weeds of mistrust and pride
that have, for so long,
uprooted any hope of authenticity

before you I was barren desert
so ruled by fears of abandonment
I abandoned others before I ever
gave them the chance to do it to me

before you I was body
bereft of the ability
to be anything but chaff
but then you

walked right into my desert

showered safety and
bloomed perseverance until
I finally quit asking you to leave

silently surrendered to your love
and told you I'd let you stay
as long as you'd like
I'd still be

stone heart
barren desert
without a hope
if it were not for you

and after spending years
asking you to leave
the least I could do is tell you
why I now spend more time

tending the garden of our relationship
planting prayers for us to grow closer
babygirl, this love letter is for you

you, who wear warrior like you
descended directly from Deborah
you, whose heart loves like
the thought of holding back
never even occurred – better yet

that it did occur and Your heart
hurdled right over it so we
could keep running this
glorious race together

I promise I am not
leaving your side
call me ride or die
because you are not competition

you are confidant, companion, comrade,
you are courageous carrier of my burdens
when the strength in my shoulders
has all but up and left

yes, I dedicate this love letter to you;
who juggle the role of sister, mother,
lover, daughter, and friend with such grace
it reminds us why it was not good
for Adam to be alone

you are not weak – you are worthy
carry tenacity in your bones
beauty in your blood
because your beautiful
is beyond skin deep

the world may tell you
you are too fat, too tall,
too short, too skinny
too much imperfect
not enough divine

but they are blind

fail to realize they get glimpses
of the very image of God
whenever they gaze
upon His daughters

your value is not measured by
the numbers that crawl around your waist
and choke the confidence out of your hips
don't you let go of that confidence, ma

your hips are divine,
curve that way
because they hold generations of home
like God knew exactly
what He wanted His children
to be carried by

your skin, tells photoshop to get lost
is beautifully blemished by bravery
littered with laugh lines
because the joy of the Lord has
always been your strength

do not cower when
these features are pointed out
stand tall and girl,
you better let them know

the world has not a clue of true beauty
is too often lost in translation because
it does not speak the language of
fearfully and wonderfully made

but you do

you, whose backbone
breaks off cowardice and unbelief
whose feet don't drag

but dance forward
wrapped in the gospel of peace
laughing because they
are not afraid of the future

you, worthy women of wonder
weave worship with wisdom
welcoming Holy Spirit's
presence with excellence

teach me worship is not
confined to four walls
but courses through
our very veins

you were never made
to be a one-size-fits-all
please, don't ever try to be!

you are too cherished
you are too needed
to be anything other than
exactly what God
created you to be

you are not left out,
never unwelcome
you are family,
you are inheritor of a living hope

possessor of heaven on earth
babygirl, you are NOT
easily thrown away

your steps drip legacy
your eyes reassure
the reality of redemption
every time we look at you

I love you, I need you,
I refuse to watch you cripple
under the weight of
satan's lies any longer

'cause baby, you, you make us better

love,
your ride or die

Made in the USA
Middletown, DE
23 August 2017